YOU ARE
MY GODDESS
ON EARTH

YOU ARE
MY GODDESS
ON EARTH

WILLIAM TAPER

Copyright © 2024 by William Taper.

Library of Congress Control Number:	2024912638
ISBN:	Hardcover	979-8-3694-2482-7
	Softcover	979-8-3694-2481-0
	eBook	979-8-3694-2483-4

All rights reserved. No part of this book may be reproduced or transmitted in any form or by any means, electronic or mechanical, including photocopying, recording, or by any information storage and retrieval system, without permission in writing from the copyright owner.

Any people depicted in stock imagery provided by Getty Images are models, and such images are being used for illustrative purposes only.
Certain stock imagery © Getty Images.

Print information available on the last page.

Rev. date: 10/28/2024

To order additional copies of this book, contact:
Xlibris
844-714-8691
www.Xlibris.com
Orders@Xlibris.com
860329

CONTENTS

You Go Your Way 1
Why Are You Leaving Me? 2
Stay With Me Tonight 3
Girl 4
You're My Godness 6
Prove It To Me 7
Love 8
Don't Lead Me On 9
Sweetness 10
I Am Closer To You 11
My Love Will Surely Grow 12
Let Me Look Into Your Eyes 13
Oh, Please Don't Cry 14
If It's Possible To Love You 15
You Miss Me 16
Give Me Your Love 17
Can You Help Me? 18
I'm Looking For You 19
Don't Wait For Me 20
Was It Really True? 21
I'm Lonely Without You 22
I Am Very Sorry 23
Can't Let You Go 24
Here I Am 25
You Can Depend On Me 26
I Can't Make It Without You 27
We Were Meant To Be Together 28

My Responsibility Is To Love You 29
Far Away 30
Please Don't Use Me 31
Stay 32
My Love Is Strong For You 33
Heather, Don't Go 34
Jennifer, Come Back 35
I Love You Natalie 36
Please Don't Go Marjie 37
I Got You Danielle 38
If You Love Me Dawn 39
Don't Leave Annie 40
Liz, You Will See 41
Karen, How Can I Love You 42
P.J. Give Me A Second Chance 43
Rhonda When You Want it 44
K.J. Put Your Hand In Mine 45
Let Me Make Love To You Angela 46
Lisa, My Love Is True For You 47
Christy, I Will Do My Best To Love You 48
They Can't Keep Us Down 49
I Was Wrong 50
I Don't Know If I Should 51
What About It 52
Perhaps 53
Am Desperate 54
You're The Best Lover I Ever Had 55
I Know You're There 56
Short, But Sweet 57
We Should Try It Again 58
Do You Wanna See Me Down On My Knees 59

The book is dedicated to my family and friends. I went to Wyman School in 1977 through 1979 and graduated with my certificate. Then I went to Roosevelt High School and graduated with my diploma. I also went to Tarkio College and graduated with certificate for childcare class. I met my niece father Mr. James Robert Lee Cotton in 1981. Mr. Cotton is my brother in law who took me under his wing. Mr. Cotton was a music producer, and Blues singer. Also my mentor until his timely death proceeding him in 2000. My ex fiancé Ms. Katheleen Marie Holloran Irish passed away in nine teen ninety-four. Then my career started, I have been writing song lyrics, song poetry 12.26.2000 25 years I enjoy it. I also grew up in church God, said to me, the minute you think you're greater, then song lyrics, song poetry, you're finished. Aka, Little, Will.

Helen
Briana
Nadine
Syliva
Irene
Sherri
Mavin
Emma Curry
Kim

William Walter Taper
Songwriter and composer

You Go Your Way

There's something I want to tell you my darling. And that is I do love you with all my heart and soul. And that will never change the way I feel about you girl.

It's hard to tell you how I really feel for you baby. You didn't no that I'm the one who really do love you honey. So, therefore I want you to please go your way, right now.

Because I can't understand why you do me wrong. Tell me what have I done to you, I his, girl I wanna know. So I can say I'm very, very sorry, it won't happen again.

Do you believe me my darling. I'm not lying to you. Honey bunch, please do me a favor and go your way. Right now because I can't stand the pain, if you leave me.

Why Are You Leaving Me?

I just wanna ask you a question, why are you leaving me girl? Is it something that I said to upset you last night baby? If so, then I'm very sorry that I hurt you baby. It won't happen again, do you here me talking to you honey?

I know you do so why don't you answer back when I call your name? What's wrong with you, I would like to know right now, girl. Because I really do need you in my life today. I'm not lying to you my darling. I really do love you forever.

I just wanna ask you a question, why are you leaving me girl? Is it something that I said to upset you last night baby? If so, then I'm very sorry that I hurt you baby. It won't happen again, do you hear me talking to you honey?

I know you do so why don't you answer back when I call your name? What's wrong with you, I would like to know right now, girl. Because I really do need you in my life today. I'm not lying to you my darling. I really do love you forever.

Stay With Me Tonight

All I want is for you to stay with me tonight, little darling. Cause I really do need you in my life forever and ever sugar. There's no one else that I want in my life but you baby. Did you here me talking to you sweet pretty thing, yes or no?

Then why don't you answer me right now? I'm waiting for your answer today girl. I promise you that I won't leave you tonight or tomorrow. Because I need you in my life right now. Would you please stay with me tonight girl?

All I want is for you to stay with me tonight, little darling. Cause I really do need you in my life forever and ever sugar. There's no one else that I want in my life but you baby. Did you hear me talking to you sweet pretty thing, yes or no.

Then why don't you answer me right now? I'm waiting for your answer today girl. I promise you that I won't leave you tonight or tomorrow. Because I need you in my life right now. Would you please stay with me tonight girl?

Girl

Girl, can't you see that I'll always love you forever. So therefore, please do me a favor and come back to me baby. Because there's no one else in the world I'd rather be with than you. Do you here me talking to you sweet pretty thing?

If you really do need me then tell me tonight baby. Because I wanna here you call my name every night little girl. Can't you see that I'll be there for you when you call my name honey. But please come back to me right away little darling, ooh, ooh.

All I want is for you to do is love me over and over. I promise you that I'll always treat you right, from now on sugar. Cause I'll do anything for you. Just give me one more chance to prove my love to you girl. There's no one else I'd rather be with than you honey.

I'm not lying to you little girl, don't you believe me sugar? If you do then please hold me in your arms tonight baby. Can't you see that I'll always love you sugar pie honey bunch. You no I love you girl. I can't help myself, I love you and nobody else.

This poem book is dedicated to my family, my friend, my fiancee, Katheleen Marie Holloran. A beautiful Irish woman who I will always love and cherish from the bottom of my heart. Even though she passed away five weeks before we were to be married. In nineteen-ninety-four on Father's Day, I made her a promise that no one else will take her place. I also apologize, if I have offended anyone by writing my book. I try to write about other people's feelings, emotion, love and as well as life. I would like to thank my Lord, my Savior, Jesus Christ, for giving me the talent to read and write poems, lyrics and songs for eighteen years. I enjoy each and every moment of it, thank you.

Sincerely,
William Taper

You're My Godness

You're my Godness because God sent you to me and I can't
let you go girl. Do you here me talking to your Father and
your Mother on the telephone today? They didn't tell you
that I called them yesterday morning and told them
that I really love you and that I will never change my
feelings for you girl. Can't you see that I will worship
the ground you walk on honey?

And that will never change the way I feel for you baby doll.
Because you are so gorgeous to me little darling.
That I can't help but to look at you forever, and ever
little girl. And don't you ever forget that I care about
you honey. And I know you care about me the same way
I care about you girl.

And I don't like at all do you here me baby yes or no.
I wonder where your ex boyfriend is hiding
at right now. So I can tell him that you are my
universe and I love you. And that will never change
my love for you girl. Because you are my Godness,
And I love you forever.

Prove It To Me

Remember one thing, little girl, I do love you from the
bottom of my heart. There's nothing I want you to do for me
my darling. And that is proof that you really love me
yes or no. Because I need to know your answer, right now.
Before I go out the front door, please prove it to me.

Because you don't love me anymore I can see it in
your eyes. Now tell me, am I wrong and you're right, I
wanna know the truth today. Not tomorrow morning
my darling, I can't wait for you to lie to me anymore.
If you don't prove it to me then let me go with my life
honey. Because I can tell that you don't love me anymore.

Girl, why did you leave me for another man?
What did I do to you sweet pretty thing?
I wanna know right now so I can make it up to you.
Would you please give me another chance to love
you girl? I promise you that I won't bite you I just
want to love you honey.

Because you are so beautiful to me I want to look
at you and no one else. Do you hear me calling out
your name in my sleep? If you do girl, then why don't
you kiss me and tell me that you love me tonight?
I promise you that I won't hurt you baby doll.
Do you understand me? Yes or no, if you do then
please prove it to me girl.

Love

I would like to thank you from the bottom of my heart.
Little girl, there's no one else that I love but you and only you. Do you hear me calling your name day and night?
Yes, you are so sweet pretty thing. I do love you forever.
And that's no lie I, his girl, I truly love you honey.

Please believe me right now I'm on my knees begging you please. Come on home to me right now because I need your love to see me free. I won't be lonely without you any more my darling. Because I am moving on with my life, do you hear me little girl? I'm moving out of your house, right now. Don't try to stop me honey.

I'm mad at you so don't get in my way because I love you.
And you love me the same way I love you, little girl.
And you will always love me forever and ever honey.
Just remember, who loves you day and night. I do.
And there's no one else you can run to for help. Just remember, I'm there for you.

Whenever you need me all you got to do is call my name.
And I guarantee that I will be there for you.
Just don't let me down, I'm counting on you my darling.
Please, let me love you with all my heart and soul.
That's all I want to do is love you forever and ever.

Don't Lead Me On

Please don't lead me on tonight, my darling, do you hear me talking to you, yes or no? I'm waiting for you to tell me that you really love me. And there's no one else in your life but me do you agree with me honey? That I'm the one for you yes or no baby? I'm waiting for you to call and tell me that you need me today.

And not tomorrow because I can't let you leave me for another man, little girl, I will do anything for you honey. All you gotta do is ask me and I will do it for you, girl. Because you are the one that I love forever and ever. And don't you ever forget that, little girl, do you hear me talking to you right now?

Baby I know you can hear me calling your name in my sleep at night. The reason why I call you name in my sleep is because I truly love you girl. And with your love I'm free from the pain I feel inside my heart for another woman. Like I told you sugar, there's no one else in my life but you and only you girl.

I'm not lying to you because I really do love you. From the bottom of my heart, let me show you how I feel about my darling. It won't take long for me to love you like I used to love you baby. All I need is for you to come home to me right now. Are you willing to do that much for me, yes or no? Don't lead me on little girl.

Sweetness

You're my sweetness in the morning and there's nothing I can
do about it honey. Would you help me get over my problem
that I have. Tell me what to do with my sweetness that I've
right now. There's no one else that I can turn to but you girl.
Did you really love me or were you just leading me on?

Like all of your friends were doing me but I don't care.
Just as long as I have you by my side I, His darling.
Are you ready to be my little girl, forever and ever?
Yes or no, I'm waiting for your answer, right now.
Do you hear me talking to you sweet sexy thing?

Yes or no, I wanna know, will you be my sweetness in
the morning? Because I do love you forever and ever
little girl. And that will never, ever change the way I
feel about you, honey. Please believe me my darling, I'm not
lying to you sugar pie honey bunch. Please come back
to me right now. I'm lonely for you girl.

Please let me make it up to you right now. Would you do
that much for me baby? I'm waiting for you to say to me
that you love me forever and ever. I'm counting on you
to love me in the morning and at night. And don't you ever
forget that sweet sexy thing. Because I'm counting
on you to be my sweetness forever and ever girl.

I Am Closer To You

It doesn't matter where you are little girl, I will always
be there for you. Because I will always care for you sweet,
pretty thing. And don't you ever forget that little darling, do you
here me talking to you? Baby, yes or no, I can't wait
for you to call me honey. If you do then let me kiss you
all over your beautiful body tonight girl.

Can't you see I am closer to you then you think my dear.
All you gotta do is look all around and you will see my face
looking at you. And I won't be smiling at all, do you here me
talking to you sugar? If you do then please, come back home
where you belong. I'm not playing with you little darling, come
back to me, OK honey?

I promise you that I won't hurt you ever again my dear.
Just give me another chance to love you forever and ever, girl.
I won't let you down today or tomorrow, do you here me baby?
I am closer to you then your ex-boyfriend will ever be.
And that will never ever change my feeling that I have for you.

Please believe me girl, I'm not lying to you anymore sugar.
Ask me anything you want to and I will tell you the truth
right now. Because I really, really care about your, forever
and ever girl. I'm not lying to you, I'm for real, with you
baby doll. Just remember one thing, I am closer to you
then you really think I am today.

My Love Will Surely Grow

Honey, there's something on my mind, I got to tell you.
And that is my love will surely grow for your baby doll.
Do you here me talking to you right now, my darling?
If you do, then answer me back with yes or no girl.
I can't wait all night for you to call me little darling.

So, therefore I'm going to find me someone else who will
love me just right. Because you don't, really, really need me
in your life today sugar. Then, why are you leading me on
little girl? I wanna know the truth right now. Before I walk
out the door and never, ever come back into your life honey.

I know you don't want that girl, do you? If so, then tell me right
now so I can kiss you all over your body tonight, little girl.
Cause I love you. And that will never, ever change the way
I feel for you sugar. So why are you playing these crazy games
with me today baby? I wanna know what have I done to
hurt you? I'm very sorry, it won't happen again.

I promise you girl, give me another chance to win your love.
I know I can do it just right this time around, little darling.
Please believe me, I'm not lying to you sweet pretty thing.
My love will surely grow for you sugar pie, honey bunch.
I'm not lying to you baby. I do love you for ever.

Let Me Look Into Your Eyes

Before we make love girl, let me look into your eyes.
Because you have beautiful green eyes. I can't help
but to look at you sweet pretty thing do you here me?
I'm talking to you little darling. Answer me back with
yes or no. I'm waiting for you baby doll.

Tell me what's wrong with you. What can I do to make
you happy? All I wanna do is look into your eyes tonight
girl. If that's ok with you sweet sexy thing, turn around
so I can look at you honey. Can't you see that I
love you forever, and ever? And that will never, ever
change the way I feel for you darling.

Please don't do me wrong. I promise you that I won't
leave you anymore. Just as long as you let me look
into your eyes tonight sugar. Please don't say no to
me little girl, cause I love you honey. Do you believe
me? Yes or no. I'm waiting for you to call me so we can
talk about us all day long until the sun goes down.

And return in the morning because we are in love.
I can feel it and so can you baby baby.
You don't have to go away from me little girl.
Because I'm trying to love you all over your body
tonight. Just do say I can look into your eyes
right now honey.

Oh, Please Don't Cry

Let me tell you something you I do love you today.
I'm not lying to you sweet pretty thing, do you here me.
Talking to you in our bedroom, yes or no honey.
I'm not playing with you, I'm for real baby.
So why don't you come on home to me right now?

Where you belong I'm waiting for you to call me girl.
I'm not going to hit you ever again. Oh, please don't
cry honey. I need you in my life, right now are you
ready to give me all of you today and tomorrow my
darling. Please say said to me, I won't hurt you in our
bedroom.

Because I really, really need your sweet tender loving.
To keep me warm at night, I know you won't bite me at
all. Let me know if you need me to do anything else, for
you babe. You know I will do anything to keep you happy
day and night. Because that's my job to keep you satisfy
forever sugar.

Just don't you walk away from me ever again, girl.
If you do then I will cry and you don't want that my
darling. So, do a favor and don't tell your family
that we made love last night. And I can't get you off
of my mine today little darling. Oh, please don't cry
I'm coming home to you tonight baby.

If It's Possible To Love You

I would like to know, is it possible for me to love you little girl?
If so, then please tell me the truth right now. I'm waiting honey.
Please don't lie to me because I really don't need you in my life
right now. Can't you see I'm crying over you and know one else
baby. If you don't believe me, then look into my eyes and you
will see my crying over you girl.

I know you love me, so why are you playing games with me?
I'm not the only one you should play games on. Play your game
with someone else. And not with me little girl, I'm too
old for playing games and you are too honey. That's why I
would like to known why is it so hard to care for you. I would
like to know the truth right now, before I walk out the door.

And never, ever come back into your life again my darling.
Do you understand where I'm coming from little darling?
I would like to know if its possible to love you all over again.
I'm willing to do whatever you want me to do, just don't leave
me sugar. I'm going to cry my eyes if you ever leave me little darling.

Don't you know that I will come looking for you sweet pretty thing?
There's nothing I wouldn't do for you. All you gotta do is ask me.
And, I will do my best to give you what you need baby doll.
That's my job, to give you what ever your little heart desires.
But there's something I need to know if it's possible to love you.

You Miss Me

Your family told me yesterday that you miss me.
Is it true honey? I wanna know right now. Do you
here me talking to you? Please answer me back
right now. I'm waiting for your answer. Please
don't make me wait too long for you to call me.
Ok, I, hie girl, I am waiting for you to kiss me.

And tell me that you really, really love me.
And there's no one else in your life but me.
Honey, please don't lie to me, I'm counting on you.
Please don't let me down I'm lonely for you girl.
Can't you see that I'm crying over you baby.

Do you really, really know what I feel inside my heart.
I don't think so. Then why are you laughing at me?
Girl, tell me the truth right now if you love me darling.
Then why don't you come back home where you belong?
I promise you that I want you any more baby.

Please believe me, I'm not lying to you little girl.
I really do care about you forever until death us
apart. I can tell that you miss me right now
because you're crying over me. Girl, please be
strong, it's not over between us, okay honey?
We must come together as one, can't you see girl?

Give Me Your Love

You know I will do anything for you sweet pretty thing.
All you gotta do is ask me and I will do my best.
To give you what you need, but there's one thing
you must do for me and that is give your love right now.
Can't you see that I'm hurting inside and outside?

For your love, please don't do me wrong little girl.
Cause I need you sugar and you need me too my darling.
Do you here me talking to you? If you do, then please answer
me back with yes or no. I'm waiting for your answer.
Don't make me wait too long sweet sexy thing.

I need you in my life today. There's no one else that I'd
rather be with than you my darling. So please give me
your love forever and ever little darling. You can't leave
without me. Just like I can't leave without you, honey.
There's one thing I got to say to you baby.
And that is I love you forever and ever girl.

But do you really, really love me the same way I love you?
I need to know the truth right now before I go honey.
And never come back into your life again baby.
I'm not playing with your feelings or emotions today.
All I want is for you to give me your love tonight.

Can You Help Me?

Here's something I want to ask you little girl. Can you help me find my way back home? Because I'm lost and I need your help right now baby. I hope and pray that you won't let me down today honey. Because I'm counting on you sweet pretty thing. Do you here me talking to you girl? Please answer me back with yes or no. I'm waiting for your answer today, sugar.

I promise you that I will be there if you need me in your life today. All you gotta do is ask me and I will do my best to give you what you need. Just as long as you help me solve my problem. Right now baby. That's all I need is for you to help me find my way back home today. Honey, cause I really need you in my life forever and ever sugar.

So why don't you help me find my way back home today little girl? I promise you that I will pay you back for helping me get home today baby. Would you please do me that favor and help me right now? I'm begging you - please don't go my dear. Would you help me before you go out the door. I'm counting on you right now babe, to come home and help me with my problem today.

I thought you could be the one I could depend on in my life, sugar. But I just was wrong to depend on you girl. It won't happen again honey because I'm going to find someone else to help me solve my problem. So therefore you don't have to come over to my house today or tomorrow baby. I'm going to tell your father if you don't help me get home today my darling.

I'm Looking For You

There's one thing I want to tell you, I'm looking for you little girl. Because I need you in my life right now. Do you here me, honey? If you do then answer me back with yes or no baby doll.
I hope you don't have another man in your life today, sugar.
If you do then I will be looking for you and you don't want that, do you girl?

Because I will be very upset with you, don't you ever forget that, girl. If you ever decide to come back to me I will be waiting for you. So I can hold you in my arms forever, and ever, my darling. And never, ever, let you go cause I love you and that will never change the way I feel for you sweet pretty thing did you here me talking to you?

I know you don't want me to cry all over, but I have to in order to show you that I love you girl. Just promise me that you won't leave me tonight, baby. If you do then I will come looking for you my dear. And you don't want that little girl because I will show you that I need you in my life forever. That's why I'm looking for you honey, because you will treat me like a man.

Suppose to be treated when no other woman will do the job right. You know how to love me baby you no you do you know how to love me baby. That's why I'm looking for you. Please don't hide from me today. Because I will never, ever, give up looking for you honey. There's one more thing I gotta say to you, I love you and I need you.

Don't Wait For Me

Girl, I'm not coming home tonight, so please don't wait up for me. Can't you see that I'm on the road tonight and I won't be home until tomorrow morning honey. So therefore all I'm asking is for you to bear with me little girl. If you want to, then please find someone else to love you. Because you don't have to wait for me to come home tonight.

If you are that lonely for someone else, I won't be mad at you honey. If you decide to cheat, then keep it to yourself, sugar. Because you have needs to fulfill and I understand. So therefore, go on fulfill your needs that you have tonight girl. Because I don't love you anymore, do you here me baby?

I'm talking to you sugar pie honey bunch. Find someone else that will love you right. Because I don't want you to wait for me anymore little girl. Go on with your life because I'm going on with my life today. Do you here me talking to you my dear? I know you do hear me honey. Don't look at me that way, I know you're mad at me but I'm very sorry if I hurt you last night.

But there's one thing you must do for me and that is go on home to your boyfriend. He's the one you love and should be with forever and ever, girl. You're wasting your time on my, can't you see I don't want you anymore, honey. That's how it's got to be so move on with your life right now. Because I don't want you to wait for me today or tomorrow, little girl.

Was It Really True?

Girl, was it really true that you are leaving me tonight? I wanna know, are you leaving me right now, sweet pretty thing? Because I need you to stay here with me forever, and ever, girl. Can't you see that I'm hurting inside and outside, for your love. Just tell me was it really true that you didn't love me sugar?

I know you're feeling sad but please forgive me little darling. Would you let me make it up to you right now, my dear? Do you need me in your life today or tomorrow sugar? If you do, then please tell me true do you really love me, yes or no? Cause I'm so lonely for you - are you lonely for me too girl?

So why don't you stop playing games with my heart and tell me the truth. Is it really true that you love someone else besides me? Yes or no? There's only one thing I need to know - was it really true my dear? That you love someone else and not me baby baby? There's only you in my life, you didn't know that honey bunch.

Please let me kiss you all over your beautiful body tonight. Please don't say no. If you do then I will cry over you girl. Because I need you and you need me in your corner. Did you here me talking to you honey bunch? I love you and that will never change my feelings for you girl.

I'm Lonely Without You

If you ever go away from me I will cry my eyes out over you girl. Can't you see I'm lonely without you baby doll, do you hear me talking to you girl? There's no one else that I'd rather be with than with you sweet pretty thing. Please believe me when I say I love you tonight honey bunch. Cause I'm not lying to you sugar pie, honey bunch. Please, believe me.

Can't you see that I will do anything to win your love right now. Just ask me and I will do my best to give you whatever you need and want, girl. Just don't leave honey bunch, I'm not playing games with you sugar. I'm for real and this is not a joke. I'm not playing with your feelings and emotions sweet pretty thing. Can't you see that I'm lonely without you little girl, did you hear me?

I'm talking to you right now baby doll. Answer me back with yes or no my dear. There's something I gotta say to you and that I'm very lonely without you. So why don't you come on home to me tonight my darling. I'm not going to hurt you anymore do you hear me honey? Cause you mean the world to me and that will never change.

The way I feel for you sweet sexy thing, I do love you. But do you really, really love me the way I love you, sugar? So let's get married today. I'm ready right now, little girl. Please don't say no, it will break my little heart, honey. And you don't want that, do you baby doll? Yes or no?

I Am Very Sorry

Girl, I am very sorry that I hit you last night in our bedroom. It won't happen again, do you hear me girl? Yes or no? Please answer me back right now baby doll. I'm waiting for your answer right now. Don't make me wait too long for you to talk to me honey bunch. I do love you forever and ever and that will never ever change the way I feel about you, girl.

That's why I'm very sorry that I hit you yesterday, girl. Can I please come back home to you honey? I'm lonely for your love today. I thought you knew that I was in love with you from the first day we met, girl. At your house I knew it was love that came over me last night in your house. Did you feel the love in the air last night, baby doll?

I would like to know right now. I can't wait for you to love me girl. That's why I'm moving on with my life today, do you hear me sugar? There's no turning back. If I leave you today, baby, I'm not lying to you, there's no coming back to you little darling. Do you hear me talking to you honey? I am very, very sorry.

That I couldn't love you better than before, baby doll. Please forgive me sugar, it won't happen again, do you hear me honey? I'm begging you to give me another chance to love you all over again. I know I will do a damn good job on you if you let me girl. I won't hurt you ever again, I promise you baby.

Can't Let You Go

There's no one thing I want to say to you little darling. I can't let you go away from me tonight baby. Because you might not come back into my life. So therefore I can't trust you to come back to me. Then I'm going to find me someone else to love me.

So therefore you don't have to come back into my life today or tomorrow. Did you hear me talking to you baby, yes or no? Please answer me back right now before I go and never come back to you girl, ever again. I'm gone for good this time, do you understand that I still love you girl? And that will never change.

The way I feel for you, do you hear me talking to you honey? If you do then answer me back with yes or no baby? I'm waiting for your answer, right now sweet, sexy thing. Please don't make me wait too long for you to call me. When you get home tonight I will be waiting for you to call.

So I can tell you something that will make your day. I know you will like it because I'm going to sing it to you girl. And I don't want you to hang up the telephone tonight. Because I can't let you go ever again little darling, do you believe me sugar? I'm not lying to you baby, please give me another to love you honey.

Here I Am

Honey, here I am waiting for you to come home tonight. So we can make sweet, sweet love all day and all night girl. Can't you see that I need you in my life right now sugar. So why don't you stop playing these crazy games with me. I don't feel like it today or tomorrow, little girl.

So why don't you leave me alone right now. I'm not playing with you, do you hear me talking to you baby? Yes or no. Please answer me back, I can't wait for your answer today. I'm moving on with my life right now so why don't you little girl. I know you're not afraid to leave me or if so just remember, here I am, waiting for you sugar.

Don't let me down. I'm counting on you to love me forever. Because there's no one else who will care for me like you do, girl. And I just wanna say to you here, I am here if you need me. Then, just call my name and I will be there in a flash. And you don't have to worry anymore. Here I am for you honey.

So stop crying right now. I mean it my darling. I don't wanna hear you crying in our bedroom. If I do then I'm leaving you for another woman. And I know you don't want that honey, do you? Yes or no? Cause I don't wanna do that to you girl, here I am for you.

You Can Depend On Me

I'm there if you ever need me in your life, little darling. Because I know you have been hurt by another man, and I'm sorry. But life goes on, just remember that baby doll. I do love you. But there's someone else out there for you so move on with your life, sugar. I will always be there if you ever need me, just call my name girl.

And I will come running to you day or night because I'm your best friend. And that will never, ever change the way I feel for you, my dear. Do you understand me little girl? I'm talking to you right now honey. Please listen to every word that I'm saying to you, sugar. I'm not going to repeat myself over and over again, baby.

Do you understand me? I want you to listen the first time and catch on to what I'm saying to you girl, because I need you in my life forever, my darling. Do you hear me girl? Before I go, there's something I gotta say to you, you can depend on me to be there for you. In good times and thru the bad times, I'm on your side, baby doll. Please believe every word that I'm saying is true and I'm not lying to you girl.

There's one thing that I want you to know, that you can depend on me. I promise you that I won't let you down ever again, do you understand me sugar? If not, tell me what have I did to upset you my darling? I'm willing to make it up to you. Just name it sweet sexy thing, and I will do whatever you want because you can depend on me.

I Can't Make It Without You

Let me tell you something girl, I can't make it without you. Honey, if you leave me then I will cry over you baby doll. So therefore would you please stay here with me my dear? I'm begging you, please don't go away from me sugar. Can't you see that we are in love with each other?

And they can't take away from us today do you hear me girl? I'm searching for someone just like you, do you understand? What I'm saying to you baby doll, I need you in my life. Honey, don't play games with my feelings or emotions, do you hear me? Girl, I'm not the one you should be playing with.

So find you someone else to play your crazy games. Cause I don't want to play today or tomorrow. I'm not in the mood for horse playing around. Didn't you hear me talking to you little darling? I know you hear me calling your name, right now.

Why can't you answer me back when I call you? Baby, you act like I'm not there when you call me. I'm willing to do whatever you want me to do, girl. All you gotta do is ask me and I will do my best to give you a good life because I can't make it without you.

We Were Meant To Be Together

Girl, you know I will always care for you no matter what happens between us. Because we were meant to be together, forever until death do us part. Can't you see that we were meant to be together forever, little girl? Please believe me. I'm telling you the truth now, my darling. Please come back to me, you know I need you in my life today and tomorrow.

And don't you ever forget that I love you from the bottom of my heart and that will always remain in my heart, forever and ever, girl. There's no one else that makes me feel the way you do my dear. That's why I love you, honey. Regardless what your family and friends might say of us, don't listen to them. Because they are jealous of us. I can tell and so can you, little girl.

Can you feel the love that I have for you in my heart?
It's burning like passion that only you can solve, honey.
So are you up to the test today? I can pass it right now.
I'm ready for your love today, do you hear me baby?
Cause we were meant to be together, forever and ever.

Do you believe me sweet, sexy thing? I care for you right now. And no one else will ever come between us, did you hear me? I'm talking to you baby doll. Please answer me back with yes or no. There's no one else that I'd rather spend my life with but you and only you. There's one thing I want to say to you that is, I love you today, tomorrow and forever.

My Responsibility Is To Love You

You know what? Let me tell you what my responsibility is to love you, girl. I know I'm right and you're wrong sweet pretty thing. I love you so therefore please let me love you all over again baby. I promise you that I won't hurt you anymore honey bunch. Do you believe me when I say I love you girl, forever?

If you do, then let me tell you my responsibility is to love you. And that will never, ever change the way I feel for you sugar. There's no one else I'd rather be with than you, baby doll. You don't have to go away from me anymore, can't you see? I love you little girl, but do you really know what my responsibility is to love you?

Day and night, sugar and that's not all I'm supposed to do for you. Let me tell you what I'm supposed to do for you honey bunch. And that is to kiss you all over your beautiful body day and night. Because we were meant to be together forever, sugar. Can't you tell that I'm lonely for you, so why don't you give yourself to me tonight.

I promise you that I won't tell a soul that we made love yesterday in our living room and it felt so good to me, let's do it again. It won't hurt either one of us if we just do it right now. I'm sure that you will see that my responsibility is to love you. And I hope and pray that you will love me the same way, too.

Far Away

Please don't far away from me tonight, little girl. Cause I really, really do need you in my life right now. Please believe me, I'm not lying to you baby doll. I don't want you to go away from me ever again. Girl, if you do then I am going to cry over you.

Day and night and I know you don't want that, do you little girl? Because your family and friends will see me cry over you today. So if you love me then don't go far away from me today my darling. If you do then I will come looking for you and you don't want that girl. Because I will be very very mad at you baby.

So why don't you stop playing these crazy games with me. Cause I'm not the one you should be playing with today. I don't feel like it today or tomorrow my darling. So why don't you just leave me and never, ever come back in my life. You know I'm just playing with you sweet pretty thing do you hear me?

Talking to you sugar pie honey bunch, yes or no? I'm waiting for your answer right now, little darling. Please don't make me wait too long for your answer. I need to know, do you want me in your life right now? There's one thing I got to tell you girl, don't go far away from me.

Please Don't Use Me

There's something I want to tell you, my dear. I saw what you did. Please don't do it again girl, because I love you honey bunch. And I know you love me too sweet pretty thing. Do you hear me talking to you? If you do then please answer me back with yes or no. I'm waiting for you little girl. Can't you see I need you in my life forever and ever my darling?

There's no one else in the world that I'd rather be with but you and only you. Please believe me sugar, I do love you forever and ever, little girl. But do you really love me the way I love you baby? I don't think so. Because you and I know there's someone else in your life besides me. I need to know right now little girl, are you cheating on me right now?

If so, what is his name so I can shake his hand for a job well done. It doesn't matter anyway if you love him or not cause I love you girl. So why don't you listen to me? I'm talking to you and no one else honey. All I need is for you to come back to me cause I'm lonely for your love girl. There's only one thing that matters to me and that's you and only you, sugar.

Do you understand me my sugar? I do need you right now, honey. If you do then please don't use me ever again do you hear me girl? Can't you see I need you in my life forever and ever my darling? You know I love you until do us apart, baby do you hear me? I mean every word I'm saying to you my darling. Please don't use me.

Stay

I just wanna ask you a question - why are you leaving me, girl? Is it something that I said to upset you last night, baby? If so, then I'm very sorry that I hurt you sweet pretty thing. Please give me just one more chance to prove my love to you. That's all I'm asking is for you to come back to me my darling.

All I want is for you to stay with me tonight, little darling.
Cause I really do need you in my life forever and ever, sugar. There's no one else that I want in my life but you and only you my dear. Why don't you come home to me right now? I'm waiting for you.

If you don't mind then let me make it up to you baby, baby. Cause I'm hurting inside and outside for your love today. I promise you that I won't leave you tonight or tomorrow. Girl, I'm in love with you and there's no one else in the world for me but you, girl. Because I wanna know, do you really love me the way I love you baby?

And I know you need me too honey. Please don't fake it ever again sugar. Because you and I were meant to be together my darling. Do you hear me talking to you girl? So, please do me a favor and stay with me tonight little darling. Would you come back to me if I cry my eyes out over you little girl? I wanna know, would you please, please stay with me tonight, honey?

My Love Is Strong For You

Honey, you know my love is strong for you, little darling. Is it magic that you have over me or is it love? I wanna know right now before I walk out the door. And never, ever come back into your life, baby. Can't you see that my love is strong for you my dear.

And that will never change the way I feel about you. I'm for real with you. I will always be in your corner. Please don't let me down tonight. I'm counting on you darling. Can't you see I need you in my life right now, sweet pretty thing? Just remember one thing, my love is strong for you tonight.

I can't hold back sugar, my feeling is strong today. Girl, there's no one else that I care about but you. Please believe me honey, I'm not lying to you baby. So why are you leaving me for another man, I wanna know the truth, what have I done to hurt you, little darling?

Whatever it is I'm very sorry that I hurt you girl. It won't happen again, I promise you that sugar. So why don't you let me love you all over your body. It won't take me long to kiss you from head to toe. I'm waiting for your answer right now honey bunch.

Heather, Don't Go

What have I done to you Heather? Please don't go. Can't you see that I'm lonely for your sweet tender loving? Can I have it, yes or no? I'm waiting for your answer. Baby please don't turn and walk out the door today. If you do then I will cry over you day and night.

Until you come back home to me Heather, there's no one else that I'd rather be with then you sweet pretty thing. Would you let me kiss you all over your beautiful body tonight? Honey I can't wait to get you home so we can make hot passionate love to one another until the sun comes up in the morning honey.

Heather, don't go, please stay here with me so we can make hot steamy love. I'm ready to start, are you baby? So let's go sugar. I know we can do it if we try little darling, do you hear me talking to you Heather, yes or no? I'm waiting for you to talk to me, don't be shy, I won't bite you honey, I promise you that little girl.

There's one thing I got to say and that is I need you. So why don't you come on home to me right now, my dear? There's nothing I wouldn't do for you my baby doll. You know that I can make sweet tender loving to you. That's all I wanna do to you Heather, is love you.

Jennifer, Come Back

How can it be Jennifer, that you are leaving me today? What have I done to upset you, whatever it is I'm very sorry. Would you please come back into my life today, little girl? I know I have messed up but I'm very angry at myself right now. And that will never, ever change the way I feel for you baby.

It's hard to express the love that I feel down deep for you. But let me tell you how it really got started. It happened like this. We fell in love with each other and that will never ever change the way I feel for you Jennifer, please don't walk away from me. If you do girl, then please come back to me right away.

Because you make me feel so good when we make hot passionate love in the morning. That's why I gotta tell the world how I feel about you baby. Please don't be mad at me for telling the world that I love you. And I want to marry you and no one else but you. Jennifer,
don't say no tonight, because I need you in my life.

And that's no lie. Please come back to me today. Can't you see that I'm lonely for you honey bunch? So why don't you come on home to me right now. This is where you belong little girl, do you hear me talking to you Jennifer, please come back to me.

I Love You Natalie

Where are you going my dear, there's something I want to tell you sugar. And that is I love you Natalie. And don't you ever forget that little girl. Because I'm willing to give you whatever you need baby doll. Please believe me darling, I'm not lying to you little girl. All I wanna do is satisfy your every need no matter what it is.

I'm willing to do it right now. I know you need someone to love Natalie. So why don't you stop playing games with me honey? I'm not the one you should be playin# with tonight. So why don't you find someone else to play your crazy games. If not, then why don't you grow up and be a young lady. I know you can do it if you want honey bunch, I'm counting on you.

Natalie, please don't let me down, sweet sexy thing. I need you in my life. There's one thing I need to know Natalie, do you really love me? Yes or no. Can't you see I'm lonely for your love little girl, so come on and give it to me right now. Because we were meant to be together forever and ever honey. There's no one else that I'd rather be with than you baby doll.

So why don't you come back to me? I'm waiting for you little girl. I promise you that I won't tell your father or mother that we are in love with each other and that will never change my feelings that I have for you little darling. Do you hear me talking to you? Please answer me back with yes or no. I love you Natalie.

Please Don't Go Marjie

Where are you going little girl? Tell me the truth. Cause I wanna know right now sweet pretty thing. What can I do to make you happy?
Just ask me. And I will do it - you know I will baby. There's something I want you to do for me, sugar.

And that is please don't go Marjie cause I love you. And that will never change the feeling I have for you. I thought you knew that you're the only one that I need in my life. So why don't you give in to me right now honey bunch? I promise you that I won't hurt you little girl, do you hear me?

Talking to you Marjie, please don't walk away from me. Girl I'm lonely for you day and night can't you see? There's nothing I wouldn't do to keep you satisfied all night. Honey, tell me what you really, really need me to do. So I can do it right now without asking any questions.

Because I'm not the one that should be asking you questions. Can't you see that we are meant for each other, didn't you know? That I will cherish you forever and ever girl. Just let me kiss you all over your beautiful body tonight. There's one thing I got to say to you, please don't go Marjie because I love you.

I Got You Danielle

Let me tell you that I got you Danielle and that's no lie. Do you hear me talking to you, I'm not laughing at you sugar. Please believe me when I say I love you forever and I'm not lying to you. Danielle your family can't keep us apart forever cause we're in love. And they can't take that from me and you girl.

Don't let them come between us ever, sweet pretty thing. There's nothing I wouldn't do for you, all you gotta do is ask me and I will do it honey. Because I need you in my life right now baby doll. So why are you playing games with my feelings and emotions? Girl, can't you see it's tearing me apart right now?

Why are you doing this to me honey? What have I done to you? Please tell me so I can apologize to you little girl. It will never happen again do you hear me talking to you? Honey, if you do then answer me back with yes or no. Don't make me wait too long for you to love me baby.

I'm not in a rush for you to love me all over again. I promise you that I won't tell your family that we made love. Because I got you Danielle and that will never change the way I feel for you sweet sexy thing. Do you really want me? Tell me so I can come over to your house right now little girl.

If You Love Me Dawn

I wanna know why are you with another man? I thought you were in love with me little girl. But I was wrong and I'm sorry if I hurt you honey. Let me make up to you some way, somehow, I know I can do it. If you will give me a chance to love you all over your body tonight, Dawn.

I know I can satisfy you whenever you call me baby. Because that's my job, to love you day and night. So don't be afraid sugar, I won't bite you at all. Do you hear me talking to you, yes or no sweet pretty thing. Why don't you leave your old flame and come on home to me right now?

Are you scared that I'm going to you in my bedroom tonight? All I wanna do is make hot, passionate love to you honey. I don't wanna stop until you scream for more then I will know that I did a damn good job on you Dawn. Because you need a real man, not a little boy to love you baby. And I'm the one who will love you forever and ever, darling.

But do you really want me in your life right now? Please let me know so I can come over to your house today. So we can come together as one are you ready girl? I am so let's go all the way to the limit. If you love me Dawn, then show me the way to go. I'm ready for your love.

Don't Leave Annie

You know it ain't right girl. Please don't leave me Annie. What have I done to hurt you? I'm very sorry my darling. Please don't cry tonight. I mean it my darling. I'm here. So therefore you don't have to leave Annie, please stay. I promise you that I won't hit you ever again, girl.

Let me make it up to you sweet sexy thing, do you hear me talking to you sugar? Please answer me back with yes or no. Don't make me wait too long for you to come back home. I'm not going to look for you anymore, little girl. Did you hear me talking to you sugar? I'm not the one you should be playing games with.

Today or tomorrow I don't feel up to it, ok little girl? Don't you know that I'm too young to play games with you? Honey, don't cry if you can't find someone to play with you. Annie, time will heal all wounds, you will see that sugar. Just don't leave me Annie, I'm begging you to stay.

Here with me today cause I love you sweet sexy thing. Come and take my hand and together we will fly on the wing of love. I'm crazy about you babe. Please don't deny it, if you would come with me because I don't want you to leave me, Annie.

Liz, You Will See

Liz, I promise you that I will treat you like a lady. Because I love you and that will never change my feelings that I have for you. Do you hear me talking to you, sweet pretty thing? If you do then please answer back right now. You don't have to go, just stay in my corner forever, sugar. Can't you see that I love you today and that will never change?

The love that I have for you, Liz, do you hear me talking to you, honey? All I wanna do is make hot passionate love to you girl. Then you will see that I'm the one you need in your life. So why are you playing games with my feelings, I wanna know right now. Is it because your husband is a business man and you don't get a chance to see him that much?

When he comes home you don't have enough time to love him, so why are you calling me? What can I do for you, sugar? Please tell me what do you really want from me today? I'm sure you can have it, don't be afraid to ask me girl. I won't bite you at all, I promise you little darling.

Just give me a chance to love you all over your beautiful white body. I promise you it won't you at all baby doll. Are you ready to make hot passionate love tonight girl, before your husband comes home next week and catches us playing around in your house. I won't tell if you won't tell baby doll. Cause I love you honey.

Karen, How Can I Love You

Tell me how can I love you sweet pretty thing? Do you hear me talking to you girl? Please answer back with yes or no. I'm waiting for your answer honey. Can't you see that I'm hurting inside and outside for your love, sugar. There's only one thing I got to say to you Karen, and that is I love you. I'm willing to learn if you will teach me the right way, honey.

I'm begging you, please show me how I can love you, girl. I wanna know the secret on how to treat you like a lady's supposed to be treated. I'm willing to try anything today if you want me to baby. Just let me when you want it so I can be ready to love you all over your beautiful body tonight.

Karen, don't hold back. Just let go and relax ecstasy. You need to. I can tell that you need to be loved all over again. Please don't deny it, it's written all over your face, honey. So why don't you stop playing games with me, I'm ready to make love to you all night long, are you ready baby doll?

I promise you that I won't hurt you at all because I love you, girl. And that will never change my feelings that I have for you Karen. Do you hear me talking to you in our bedroom? Yes or no. All I wanna do is love you all over your beautiful body tonight. Please don't tell me to stop because I don't wanna stop until you scream for more Karen, cause I love you.

P.J. Give Me A Second Chance

P.J. give me a second chance to love you. It's not hard to do if you just give me your love tonight. I promise you that I will love you forever, baby. So why don't you kiss me once and tell me that you love me sugar. I'm waiting for your answer right now honey bunch. Please don't make me wait too long to love you all night long.

P.J. did you hear me? I'm talking to you baby doll, yes or no. Just stay in my corner, you don't have to go away sugar. I'm begging you, please don't go, I will do anything if you stay here with me right now, sugar. Would you do that much for me, girl? Because I love you and there's no one else that I'd rather be with then you honey.

Did you hear me talking to your right in our living room? Just give me a second chance to care about you my darling. I promise I won't hurt you ever again baby. I'm willing to stick by your side night and day, honey. Please believe me when I say I love you, my darling.

I'm not lying to you P.J. I really do love you from the bottom of my heart. When I look into your beautiful brown eyes I see love and desire. And that tells me that you love me forever and ever, baby. So stop playing with my feelings and emotions right now, girl. I mean it, stop playing with my feelings before someone gets hurt, girl.

Rhonda When You Want it

Rhonda, tell me when you want it tonight or tomorrow, girl. Because I'm in love with you babe, do you hear me sugar? So why don't you stop playing games and let me love you all over your beautiful white body tonight. I don't wanna stop until you scream for more then I will know that I did a damn good job on you honey. That's all I wanna do is make hot passionate love to you, baby.

Please don't say no tonight. I really do mean it, sugar. When you want it right now or later on my darling. Rhonda, I will do my best to give you whatever your heart desires. All you gotta do is let me make hot passionate love to you all over your body tonight. Honey please don't say no to me, I need you right now in my life.

Rhonda, don't walk away from me, little darling. But it is really what you want from me right now. That is love if you can handle it, little girl. Let me know right now before I start kissing you all over your body. Rhonda, ready for whatever you got to give me right now.

So come on and show me that you love me forever, honey. Just don't let me down. I'm counting on you little girl. To love me all over my beautiful black body tonight. I'm ready for us to make hot passionate love to one another. Do you hear me Rhonda, when you want it tonight.

K.J. Put Your Hand In Mine

Let me tell you something right now, darling. I can't lose you sugar. If I do then I'm going to cry. And you don't want that do you honey, cause I love you. And I know you love me the same way I love you baby. There's one thing you can do for me, let me hold you real

tight and never, ever let you go away from me. K.J., put your hand in mine right now, do you hear me talking to you in our bedroom? If you do then answer me back. With yes or no, I'm not playing games with you little girl. Let's go home where you belong, honey bunch.

If there's anything you want from me, just ask. And I will do my best to give you whatever you need. Just don't cry anymore, please baby doll. You know that I will die for you and that's no lie. Please believe me girl, I'm telling you the truth.

I wouldn't lie to you sweet sexy thing cause I need you in my life. All I want is for you to love me once again like you used to. Before we break up and go our separate ways and never come back to each other again, baby. We miss each other. Can't you tell that we are meant to be together?

Let Me Make Love To You Angela

I can't wait to get you home Angela so I can make love to you honey. Because I need you in my life right now, do you hear me talking to you girl? If you do, then please answer me back with yes or no. I can't wait no longer on you, I'm ready to make love to you Angela, because you are so sweet and tender.

All over your body I can't help but to love you day and night. Please don't tell me to stop because you will hurt my feelings. And you don't want that, do you little girl, I can't tell. That you are ready to make hot passionate love until the morning, little girl. You can't run and hide from me anymore baby.

I have you where I want you and that's in my bedroom tonight. And you get out until we make each other holler for more. Then I will know that we are both satisfied tonight, do you hear me talking to you girl? I'm for real, I'm not lying to you sweet pretty thing. I know there's no one else that can love you like I can.

All I want is a chance to love you all over your beautiful body tonight. I know I can do a damn good job on you baby. Are you willing to let me make love to you honey bunch? I promise you that I won't hurt you in our bedroom tonight. Cause you will always be my number one girlfriend.

Lisa, My Love Is True For You

There's one thing I want to tell you and that is I love you girl. But do you really want me in your life today, little darling? Let me know right now so I can come over to your house right away sugar. Because your ex-boyfriend don't love you anymore, I thought he told you last night in his apartment at least that's what he told me.

I don't believe him, I believe he's a big liar. Lisa, just remember that my love is true for you. Whenever you decide to leave your ex-boyfriend, remember that I'm the one you need in your life today. Because I am willing to love you all over your body tonight.

You know you need it so don't deny it, girl. I won't hurt you because I'm not like your ex-boyfriend, I'm the one you need in your bedroom tonight honey. So don't say you don't want me to make hot passionate love to you Lisa. Please don't tell me to stop until you get enough of love from me sugar. That's all I wanna do is treat you right, from now on.

I know I can handle it, just give me a chance to love you all over your beautiful body tonight, baby doll. I promise you that it won't hurt you tonight, girl. If you let me do it just right, it won't feel odd at all. But you will get a good felling out of it, baby.

Christy, I Will Do My Best To Love You

There's something on my mind and I need to tell you girl. So sit down and listen to what I have to say to you. It's very important that you listen to every word that I say to you Christy. Because I love you from the bottom of my heart, do you hear me talking to you, honey? There's nothing I won't give you, all you gotta do is ask me.

And I will do my best to give you whatever you need. That's why I need to no Christy. I love you forever, tell me now. So I can learn from you in order to do a good job on you baby doll. I promise you that I won't hurt you even though you're younger than me. Age is only a number to me, just remember that I love you, little girl.

And that will never change my feelings that I have for you. Please believe me when I say I do love you forever and I mean it from the bottom of my heart. I thought you knew that I cared about you and no one else, I do care about you honey. All I wanna do is kiss you all over your beautiful white body. Please don't say no to me, it won't hurt you at all, Christy. I promise you that much.

So are you ready for me to kiss you from head to toe? Let me know when I can start kissing you all over your soft and tender body tonight. It's going to take me all night long to love you baby doll. So don't get up, just relax and let me look at you all night long, my darling. Before I start to cry and you don't want that, do you little girl?

They Can't Keep Us Down

Girl, you know that I love you, until death us do part. But there's one thing I got to say to you, your father. And your they can't keep us down cause we're in love with each other. And that will never, ever change the love that have for each other. Do you hear me talking to you little darling, yes or no?

Please answer me back right now, I'm waiting for you to talk sugar. It doesn't matter if you decide to talk today or tomorrow. Just as long as you talk to me my dear, do you hear me? If you do then please tell them right now that they can't stop us from falling in love with one another, are you ready to go girl?

Let me know so I can pick you up in my brand new Ford car. Because I love you and I wanna show you the world. If you let me do that much for you sweet pretty thing. Like I said to you last night, they can't keep us down. I promise you that much just have faith in me honey bunch.

I promise I won't let you down ever again, little darling. Please believe in me, I'm counting on you to trust in me. Baby, I'm the only one that you have in your life. Besides your father and your mother, that love you. Like I told you before, they can't keep us down, baby.

I Was Wrong

There's something I want to tell you little girl. Are you ready to hear what I've to say to you baby. Am very sorry that I hurt you my darling would you please forgive me.

It won't happen again, I promise you that honey bunch.
It won't ever happen again because I was wrong. And you were right last night, I can't doubt you baby.

Would you please forgive me, I was wrong and that I know honey.
Am very sorry that I have done you wrong sweet pretty thing.
Let me make it up to you in any way that I can am willing.

To make you very happy and content do you hear little girl.
When I say I love you I really mean it from my heart darling.
Please believe me am not lying to you I promise you my love.

It won't happen again will you give me another chance.
To prove my love to you baby will you let me show you.
That you mean the world to me and there's no one else.

That I need but you and only you am for real with you.
This time but don't make me change my mind because you, forever, you know that I am the only man for you and don't you ever forget that my love, I was wrong to leave you.

I Don't Know If I Should

That's why am going to find me someone else that I can depend on. Because you're no good for me little girl, so stop pretending to be honey.
It won't work with me this time. I know your game, what you're about.

Why didn't you tell me your ways what was wrong with you.
Baby please tell me right now so we can work it out together.
That's what am here for, did you know sweet pretty thing.

I need you forever in my life please believe me sugar.
Let me know what you want out of life. I know what I want and that is you. Are you ready to be my wife forever until death do us part.

Please don't say no little girl, do you hear me talking to you.
Then why don't you answer me back with yes or no. Am waiting for you to talk to me right now darling.

Don't make me wait too long for you to give me my answer honey.
Here I am in your forever I don't know if I should be here with you. But I don't care. Just as long as we are together forever.

Just put your trust in me I won't let you down you will see baby.
That's all I need right now so give it here am in of rush at all.
So don't ask me to because am going to say no to you honey.

What About It

Give me your love forever little girl, cause I love you right now. Are you ready to give me what I need from you girl. If you can handle what I have to give you tonight.

Then show me what you are talking about my darling. I think you are afraid of me baby, can you take what I have to give you sugar. You know I love you there's no doubt that I do love you little girl.

That's why am coming home to you so we can work out our problem. That we have in our lives today little girl I don't you agree with me, baby. I sure hope so because I love you forever, and ever girl.

I wanna know your feeling and emotion that you have for me. Girl, tell me am wrong and you're right, what about it baby. Tell me now before I got to sleep tonight, tell me what's on your mind, little girl.

I wanna know your feeling and emotion that you have for me honey. Tell me am wrong and you're right, what about it girl. Is it something that you really need from me baby.

Am waiting for you to please tell me the truth baby. I won't be mad at you for telling me how you feel about me honey. Is it true love or not, I need to know right now.

Perhaps

The reason why I'm calling you is to ask you do you still love me. Perhaps not. Then am sorry if I call your house yesterday. It won't happen again, I promise you that my darling.

Please believe me sweet pretty thing. I love you baby. But do you still love me the way I love you forever. Am not in a rush for you to give me my answer today.

Take your time and think about it and tell me what you want in life. So I can give it to you sweet pretty thing. Don't hesitate to ask for what you want. I won't be mad at you for asking me and know one else my darling.

You suppose to ask me and not your ex boyfriend. Perhaps you forgot. That am your man forever and ever don't you forget that girl. Did you hear every word that am saing to you. I sure hope so.

Cause I don't like to repeat myself over and over again. Don't you agree little girl, please say yes right now baby. I know you can talk cause I heard you talking to your friend on the phone.

Don't deny it little girl, I saw you with your girl friend last night. Perhaps I was wrong but am sorry that I lied on you girl. Please give me one more chance to love you baby.

Am Desperate

Can't you see that I truly love you from my heart. Please believe me when I say I love you forever. Am telling the truth I do need you in my right now.

Girl, don't walk away from me anymore am sorry. Please give me another chance to love you Renee. I won't let you down anymore you can count on me darling.

If I do then you can put me out of house. Whenever you do Renee, I won't beg you to take me back you can bet on that darling.

Because you know am desperate to have you in my life forever. Did you hear me calling your name in my sleep at night. Don't wake me up unless you really love me from your heart.

And that will never change the way I feel about you girl. I thought you knew that yesterday when I called your name.
Please come and see what I want because am desperate.

To have you in my life right now sugar pie honey bunch. Your the only one that I need to be with. There's no one else that I'd rather be with you Renee. Even if you don't want to be with me, I still want to be with you girl.

You're The Best Lover I Ever Had

Just in case you didn't hear me darling, You're the best lover I ever had, don't you forget girl. OK, cause I love you forever and ever.

And that will never change my feeling that I have for you honey. Neither will it stop me from loving you from my heart. Am for real with you are you for me baby.

There's only you in my life so don't worry at all. Am coming home to you so we can be together forever.
My darling are you ready then here I come open the door.

Right now am waiting for you to let me in so I can tell you. That I love you and only you little girl. Cause you're the best lover I ever had in my life.

Don't you ever forget that sugar pie honey bunch.
I love you forever and ever little girl, please believe me.
I know you will do anything to keep me happy and content.

It's the truth baby please believe me am telling you the truth. I do love you my darling that's why you're the best lover I ever had in my life. It's the truth I do love you my darling. It won't change the way I feel about you baby.

I Know You're There

Honey I know you're there watching me sweetheart. I don't mind it one bit that you are watching me baby. I get a rush when you are watching me honey.

There's only you that I need in my life forever and ever. And I know you want me in your life forever and ever girl. So don't lie to me if you are for real about our love.

That we have together don't you love like I love you girl. That's what you tell me last night, my darling. I love you. I thought you knew that I need you in my life forever.

Please don't change your mind now it's too late for you to go back, on your promise. I know you're there don't hid from me ever again little darling. If you do then I will be very upset with you and you don't want that honey.

I know you don't want me to leave you for someone else, please say no. Am waiting for you to tell me that I love you forever baby. There's nothing you can't have from me you know that girl.

So don't pretend that you don't love me anymore honey. I know you're there when I call your name girl. Please answer me back right now I know you're there.

Short, But Sweet

Girl, you know that you are short but sweet that's why I love from my heart. And that will never change the way you feel for me girl. Don't lie to your friend about our love that we together.

I don't care if the whole world knows that I love you my darling. It's the truth I truly love you from my heart. And that will never change the love I have for you baby.

Neither will it stop me from giving you anything you want, sugar. All you gotta do is ask me and she'll receive it from me. Don't wait too long to ask me for what you need my love.

Am there for you honey. Please believe me little girl. So I can thank you for being there when the chips are down. You bring me up when I'm feeling down and out.

I just wanna thank youfor doing that for me. If there's anything you ever need don't hesitate to ask me. And I will do my best to give you whatever you need.

You can count on that girl, am the only man that you will ever need in your life. Don't you ever forget that my love because you're short but sweet, to me. That's why I love you forever and ever, little girl.

We Should Try It Again

There's something I want to ask you, it's very important honey. Please, sit down and listen to what I have to say to you. It's nothing bad so don't worry your pretty little head.

About it girl, I need to know do you love me yes or no. Please tell me the truth right now baby don't leave me. For another man if you do then I will cry over you honey.

And you don't want that little darling. Please say. Am waiting for my answer from you can't you talk to me. I sure hope you can sugar because we should try it again.

Are you ready to start all over again I think we should do that. It's not a problem with you is it honey. Let me know. So we can talk about it before we start dating each other.

That's all we need is true love from each other. Don't you agree sweet pretty thing yes or no. Am waiting for you to please say something to me.

Right now sugar pie honey bunch I love you forever. That's the truth honey am not lying to you baby. I do love you that will never change the way I feel about you my darling.

Do You Wanna See Me Down On My Knees

You're not convinced that is enough.
I put myself in this position and I deserve the imposition. But you don't even know I'm alive and this pounding in my heart.

Just won't die. I'm burning up for your love. You're always closing your door that make me want you more. I cry day and night for your love little girl, you're not convinced.

That's enough to justify my love for you honey bunch. Please tell me what you want me to do baby. Be right now. Because I'm not blind and I know that you still love me Carla.

That's why I can't let you get away from me anymore. Please don't make me get down on my knees. Are bending over backward for you Carla.

Because you are different, unlike the others. I would do anything to keep you happy and content. I'm not ashamed of you honey. I just want to love you forever and ever.

There's no doubt that we belong together forever. My love don't agree with me little girl. I hope so. Because I do love you forever and ever.

Milton Keynes UK
Ingram Content Group UK Ltd.
UKHW041329301124
451950UK00013B/144/J